CHINESE
FASHIONS

Ming-Ju Sun

DOVER PUBLICATIONS, INC.
Mineola, New York

Bibliographical Note

Chinese Fashions is a new work, first published by Dover Publications, Inc., in 2002.

International Standard Book Number

ISBN-13: 978-0-486-42053-0
ISBN-10: 0-486-42053-1

Manufactured in the United States by Courier Corporation
42053106   2015
www.doverpublications.com

Publisher's Note

The People's Republic of China has a recorded history of over 4,000 years. This book covers approximately 1,400 years, depicting men's and women's costumes of six distinct periods—five dynasties: the Tang (618–907), the Song (960–1279), the Yuan (1279–1368), the Ming (1368–1644), and the Qing (pronounced *Ching*; 1644–1911), and the Republic Period (1911–1949).

The **Tang Dynasty** was characterized by a curiosity about other cultures, such as Persia. Women wore high-waisted, low-necked, full-cut gowns, some with flowing sleeves; Persian-style slippers can be seen on pages 1 and 7. During the **Song Dynasty**, necklines generally were higher and gowns less voluminous. Costume of the **Yuan Dynasty** was influenced by the Mongols—rulers of China for nearly a century—in the *del*, a simply cut wrap-style garment that closed on the wearer's right. The **Ming Dynasty**, lasting almost three hundred years, saw some further changes in costume, including the shoulder cape (page 24) and long tunic (pages 25 and 27). The **Qing Dynasty** marked the beginning of the influence of the Manchu—nomadic warriors who dominated the country from 1644 until 1911—on the Han people, the major Chinese ethnic group. Manchu garments were designed for ease and comfort in horseback riding. The Manchu influence can be seen in the "horsehoof" cuff, shown on pages 37 and 39. In addition, Manchu-style loops and toggle fasteners permeated Han Chinese costume. Similarly, the Manchu adopted Han-style garment borders. Whereas female workers and young women of the Han group wore trousers, Manchu women did not. Finally, simplicity and practicality were the dominant themes of dress during the **Republic Period**—a radical departure from the elaborate designs of traditional Chinese costume. Sources of information about Chinese costume include actual garments in museums and private collections; representations of garments in watercolor paintings, and, more recently, photos; and literary descriptions.

Chinese costume is known for its stunning embroidery depicting symbols of Chinese culture. In fact, the designs and patterns acted as a sort of code, enabling the wearer to transmit information. For example, the "Twelve Symbols" served as insignia for the reigning emperor and empress and their immediate family. These symbols included the sun, moon, and stars, as well as dragons. Embroidered symbols eventually lost their significance and became purely ornamental. (Interestingly, contemporary Western clothing has adopted Chinese symbols in fashion items such as T-shirts and body tattoos.) The familiar "dragon" robe—known in the West as the mandarin robe—generally was worn by men but could be worn by women as well. These formal robes were the privilege of those who had an elevated place in Chinese society. Silks such as damask and brocade were favored by the wealthy and ruling classes; cotton was the rule for the rest of the population.

Like the sari, the draped garment traditionally worn by women in India, the Chinese robe indicated the wearer's position in society. For example, the use of embroidered dragons, one of the most popular traditional motifs, reflected the wearer's status: the more dragons on an imperial court official's robe, the higher his rank. Another indication of status was the square insignia, or rank, badge (see pages 33 and 39). In use by the Qing rulers, rank badges were codified by Emperor Ch'ien Lung in 1759 in his work *The Illustrated Catalogue of Ritual Paraphernalia of the Qing Dynasty*. This guide specified exactly who could wear a particular emblem. Civil officials displayed emblems of birds, which ranked them higher than military officers, who were restricted to emblems of animals.

The costumes in this book display a number of significant motifs and patterns, some of them from traditional groupings such as the Twelve Symbols of Sovereignty, the Eight Buddhist Symbols of Good Fortune, and the Eight Precious Objects. The dragon, one of the Twelve Symbols of Sovereignty, evoked the divine power, authority, and wisdom of the emperor. The Tang Dynasty emperor shown on page 8 wears a robe that is embroidered with a dragon motif. On page 12, a scholar wears a robe bordered with a knot pattern. This knot, known as the "mystic dragon," suggests longevity and eternity because of its endless nature. It was one of the Eight Buddhist Symbols of Good Fortune. On page 13, the woman on the right wears a robe embroidered with pairs of birds, perhaps phoenixes, which symbolized beauty, goodness, and prosperity. The lotus flower, a symbol of purity, adorns the skirt of the costume on page 35.

Other commonly used symbols were natural elements such as waves, mountain peaks, and clouds; flowers, especially peonies and chrysanthemums; birds, including the crane, the phoenix, the pheasant, and the egret; and abstract patterns representing concepts such as luck, longevity, and eternity. Color had great significance as well. Imperial rules decreed that the emperor and his immediate family were the only ones permitted to wear a bright yellow garment. In Chinese symbolism, yellow signified the directional "center," and the emperor was indeed the center of the society.

It is worth noting that Chinese costume was loose-fitting, flowing, and easy to wear, compared to the uncomfortable, restrictive clothing and undergarments, such as the corset, the crinoline, and the bustle, that became popular in the West. (Of course, the practice of foot-binding, adopted by the Han Chinese but not by the Manchu, was more painful than the most extreme style of Western shoe.) Until the late twentieth century, Chinese fashion was not designed to display the female figure. The final plate in this book shows a Republic Period dress—the *cheong sam* [chon sam], or *qi pao* [chee pow]—that reveals the contours of the body. This popular style features a high-necked (mandarin) collar, fitted waist, and side slits.

Tang Dynasty (618–907). This upper-class woman wears a strapless high-waisted dress under a transparent robe. The robe is secured by a knotted sash. She carries a fan, a popular accessory. Her hairstyle was known as "hundreds of flowers"; hairpins and other implements were used to construct the elaborate hair arrangement. The curled-toe slippers show a Persian influence.

1

Tang Dynasty. These women of the imperial palace wear the popular dress of the day—a high-waisted dress with full, flowing skirt. The long scarves that they have draped over their shoulders flow down their backs. The woman on the right wears the "double bun" hairstyle; both hairstyles are adorned with ornaments containing precious gems.

2

Tang Dynasty. This musician performs for a formal occasion at the palace. Her high-waisted full skirt is tied with a long, flowing sash. Ornaments and a bow decorate her hair.

Tang Dynasty. This young woman's loose robe is held in place by a wide sash wrapped around her hips and securely knotted. Her hair has been divided into two sections, twisted, and fastened with barrettes.

Tang Dynasty. This Tang general is shown in fur-trimmed leg armor worn over elaborately decorated boots. He wears a headdress and has tied a scarf around his shoulders. His flowing skirt allows for freedom of movement.

Tang Dynasty. A Tang official wears a hat denoting his rank as a civil servant. His simply cut robe is held at the waist by a belt.

Tang Dynasty. This upper-class woman from the later Tang period wears a high-waisted dress featuring extremely wide sleeves. Her hair is held in place by a variety of hairpins. Her turned-up shoes are made of embroidered silk.

Tang Dynasty. This Tang emperor wears an ankle-length, full-skirted robe fastened with a belt that is decorated with gold and precious gems.

Song Dynasty (960–1279). These upper-class women wear outfits consisting of a robe, skirt, long scarf, and embroidered silk shoes. The scarves fall low on the figure. Both wear their hair padded to achieve the preferred shape and height. Their hairstyles are decorated with ornaments made of gold and gemstones. They wear upturned embroidered slippers.

Song Dynasty. These military men wear outfits consisting of layers in different lengths, worn with a tunic and trousers. Both wear boots and caps. Their swords, arrow bags, and bows are suspended from their belts.

Song Dynasty. This upper-class woman wears a narrow-sleeved wrap top over an undershirt. The long skirt is held at the waist by an embroidered pocket. The long scarf serves as a shawl. Her "double bun" hairstyle is adorned with jewels and clasps.

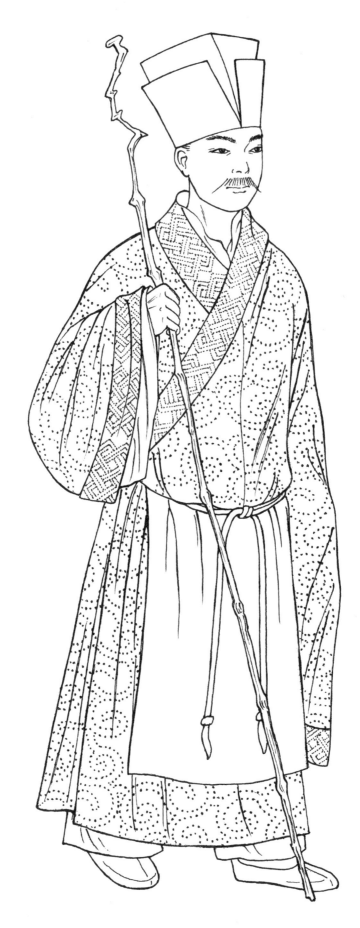

Song Dynasty. This scholar, known for his paintings and calligraphy, wears a simple wrap coat bordered with a band decorated with a "knot" pattern. An apronlike scarf drapes the front of his coat, which is held in place by a cord.

Song Dynasty. This woman and young girl are members of an imperial official's household. The woman wears a high-waisted skirt over a robe, as well as a flowing shawl-like scarf. She obviously belongs to the noble class, as the extremely long sleeves of her gown would make any sort of work impossible. The girl wears an abbreviated wrap skirt over her long robe, which displays the popular "double bird" motif. The open side seam reveals several under-skirts. The girl carries a massive fan, and both wear decorative hair ornaments.

Song Dynasty. This woman's wrap top has a neckband embroidered with a floral design. The pocket at the skirt's high waist is also embroidered with colorful silk thread. The knotted ornamental sash flows downward to flutter with her every movement. She holds a pleated fan.

Song Dynasty. These upper-class women wear closely fitted jackets with narrow sleeves. The short wrap skirt worn by the woman on the left is paired with a long skirt. The woman on the right displays a low neckline under her jacket. Embroidered bands of floral designs decorate the front, sleeves, and hems of both jackets. The women's embroidered silk hair ornaments are embellished with jewels and gold or silver details.

Song Dynasty. This commoner wears everyday attire consisting of a wrap robe and a high-waisted long skirt circled at the waist by a knotted sash. Her single-bun hairstyle is decorated with a simple ribbon.

16

Song Dynasty. This commoner's robe is brought upward and tucked in at the waist for ease in walking. The pants have been shortened as well. Sandals and a hat made from a piece of cloth complete this outfit.

17

Yuan Dynasty (1279–1368). This Yuan military officer wears a hat that has been equipped with armor to protect the back of his head and neck. Other components of his armor include an elbow-length cape, a waist and hip panel, and leg protectors. His trousers are tucked into his boots.

Yuan Dynasty. The abbreviated wrap skirt was another form of dress popular during this era. The wrap top, worn over a long-sleeved blouse, features elbow-length sleeves. One of the woman's sashes has a bow decorated with semi-precious stones. Her hair ornament is also decorated with gemstones.

19

Yuan Dynasty. This upper-class woman wears a wrap tunic with double bands of embroidered design at the opening, sleeve, and hem. Her hat, made of silk, has been decorated with embroidery and gemstones. Her hairstyle was created using barrettes and a jeweled headpiece.

Yuan Dynasty. A military officer wears a one-piece outer coat, stitched in the middle section and buttoned at the side. His hat is trimmed and lined with fur; his leather boots are decorated with braiding and embroidery. A small pouch hangs from the midriff piece.

Yuan Dynasty. Shown here are two actors in a play. The actor on the left wears a beard, signaling to the audience that he is portraying an older man. His costume features elaborately embroidered bands on the shoulders, as well as the front, hem, and sleeves of the gown. The actor on the right is dressed in a long belted gown. Some actors had extra-long sleeves, which they waved for emphasis while performing; the sleeves also added extra eye appeal during a dance interlude.

Ming Dynasty (1368–1644). The musician wears a hat with bells sewn to it. His robe is tied at the waist with a wide sash. The corner of a scarf hangs down his back, ending in a decorative tassel. He wears boots.

Ming Dynasty. Both of these upper-class women wear shoulder capes. The cape on the right features the "cloud design," consisting of round pieces of rabbit fur and embroidery. The cape on the left is decorated with crane and cloud designs. The high-necked collars have handcrafted closures.

24

Ming Dynasty. This Ming general is dressed in a long outer tunic with wide decorative bands on the sleeves and on the tunic's front and side openings. The tunic is finished with a long fringe. The general's trousers have been tucked into his boots. A hat completes the outfit.

Ming Dynasty. This general is dressed in full body armor and a helmet. The armor's front and upper sleeves and leg protectors are decorated with menacing dragon faces. Dragons represented the imperial throne (with five claws rather than the typical four) and also stood for luck. The main parts of the body armor consisted of bronze "scales" backed with a silk lining.

Ming Dynasty. This woman is dressed in a popular outfit of this period. The long-sleeved tunic has embroidered bands at the neck and sleeves. The square neckline of the outer vest is accented with a large pin. The skirt has a front panel edged in satin and floral embroidery.

Ming Dynasty. This street vendor's outfit consists of a simple wrap outer robe, an undershirt, loose trousers, and a waist sash. He has wrapped strips of cloth around his legs and feet for warmth and protection. His robe and trousers are made of solid-color cotton. His shoes also are cotton.

Qing [pronounced *Ching*] Dynasty (1644–1911). These young household workers wear simple hairstyles that flow down their backs. Both wear a long, side-slit cotton skirt, tied at the waist with a sash, over a long underskirt. They have rolled up their sleeves for work.

Qing Dynasty. This Tibetan man wears an outer robe wrapped at the side and held together with a simple sash; he wears an undershirt and long trousers beneath the robe. His accessories include a sword, a long strand of beads (probably *trengwa*, Tibetan prayer beads) wrapped around the body, and a traditional hat.

Qing Dynasty. This street vendor protects her hair with a piece of cloth wrapped around and tied into a makeshift hat. The solid-color jacket and skirt are made of cotton. She has tied a simple sash around her waist. The bag tied to the pole is made from a piece of cloth and will function as a shopping bag.

Qing Dynasty. Shown here is a lady-in-waiting at the imperial palace. She wears a silk headband decorated with embroidery and semi-precious stones. Her long silk jacket, edged with decorative bands, is worn as the outer layer over several silk garments. The collar buttons, typical of Manchu-style garment closures, might have been made of gold, silver, jadeite, or coral.

Qing Dynasty. This court official and his wife wear embroidered squares—insignia, or rank, badges whose color and motif [birds, shown here] identify the couple's status. The bead necklaces might have been made of coral, jadeite, agate, ivory, amber, or tourmaline. Both wear long toggle-closure vests. Her ornate headdress is decorated with strands of beads.

Qing Dynasty. This court musician wears a vest trimmed and lined with fur over a narrow-sleeved undershirt. The wide pant legs are decorated with embroidered ribbons. Her hair is worn in the neatly and elegantly combed "small head" style. Her earrings are of gold and precious stones such as jade or pearl. The silk shoes are embellished with embroidered flowers and leaves.

34

Qing Dynasty. This young commoner's hairstyle was known as the "loose fringe," a smoothly combed style with bangs. Her everyday outfit consists of a silk jacket decorated with embroidered ribbons, worn over a pleated silk skirt with embroidered front panel. Both the jacket and the skirt have wide embroidered bands. She wears embroidered slippers.

Qing Dynasty. This woman is the wife of a high official at the imperial court. She wears a full-length dress with a matching short vest, both decorated with gold embroidery, ribbons, and silk braiding. The high-necked vest has Manchu-style toggle closures. She wears a tall hat with a floral decoration.

Qing Dynasty. This official wears a riding jacket with the "python" design. His full-length robe has sleeves ending in "horsehoof" cuffs, a feature of the horse-riding ruling Manchu culture. The embroidered pouches with silk cords and tassels, seen dangling from his waist, held per-sonal items such as eyeglasses, a fan, or tobacco leaves. His wife's hair, adorned with jewels, is worn in the "top bun" style. Her long jacket has a circular embroidered design; the jacket is worn over a pleated silk skirt.

Qing Dynasty. These upper-class women display the "double bun" hairstyle, secured with bands and pins. The woman on the left wears a shoulder cape fastened with gemstone buttons on the high collar. The woman on the right is dressed in a jacket with embroidered bands at the square neckline. Her collar buttons are also made of gemstones. Both wear pleated skirts with embroidered front panels.

Qing Dynasty. The square insignia, or rank, badge on this official's jacket indicates his official standing. The jacket's sleeves, in the Manchu-influenced "horsehoof" shape, are folded back to form cuffs.

Republic Period (1911–1949). Both women wear long, narrow tunics with side slits and handmade button closures of silk cording. The woman on the left has a high-necked collar, encircled with bead necklaces. She wears the tunic over a pleated skirt. The woman on the right has a fur collar atop her tunic; the tunic is worn over a front-pleated skirt. Her silk headband is embellished with gold braiding, jewels, and embroidery. She wears a bangle bracelet.

Republic Period. This woman's full-length dress is decorated with bands of ribbon embroidered with colorful floral motifs done in silk, gold, and silver thread. She wears her hair in the elegant "small head" style. The dress has handcrafted button closures at the collar and along the front edge.

Republic Period. The short, fitted jacket worn by the woman on the left has wide sleeves, a rounded hem, and is edged in silk binding. The large floral designs are embroidered in silk thread. The brocade jacket on the right has narrow sleeves and an allover floral pattern. Gold and silver threads have been worked into the skirts' embroidery. Both young women wear the "loose fringe" hairstyle.

Republic Period. This knee-length dress reflects a more modern approach to women's clothes, displaying a shorter, more revealing silhouette than previous Chinese garments. Known as a *cheong sam* [chon sam], or *qi pao* [chee pow], this popular twentieth-century style has handcrafted button closures at the collar and down the side. Embroidered bands define the dress's hem and sleeves. The floral design on the dress is embroidered with silver, gold, and colored thread.